THE
BREAKUP
OF THE
SOVIET UNION

Bernard Harbor

new
Discovery
B·O·O·K·S
New York

Conflicts

Titles in the series:
The Breakup of the Soviet Union
Conflict in Eastern Europe
Conflict in Southern Africa
Conflict in the Middle East

Cover: Demonstrators clash with Soviet soldiers as tanks patrol the streets of Moscow in the attempt to restore order during the coup of August 1991.

Title page: Over 40 years after it came under Soviet rule, Lithuania gained its independence in 1991.

Picture acknowledgments
The publishers would like to thank the following for supplying their photographs for use as illustrations in this book: Camera Press Ltd. 14, 19, 22, 23, 31, 42, 43: Chapel Studios 21: Mary Evans Picture Library 7 (Alexander Meledin Collection): John Frost Historical Newspaper Service 39: Novosti Information Agency 8 *left*, 9, 10, 28; Popperfoto 11, 30 (Reuter), 38, 44 (AFP): Rex Features *Title page*, 4, 5, 13, 17, 20, 25 *top*, 26 (Sipa Press); 29 (Laski): Topham Picture Library 18 (Financial Times); *Cover*, 8 *right*, 16, 27, 32, 33, 35, 36, 37, 40, 41, 45 (Associated Press); Wayland Picture Library 6, 25 *bottom*.
The map artwork on pages 15 and 34 was supplied by Peter Bull.

Editor: Judy Martin
Series editor: William Wharfe
Designer/Typesetter: Malcolm Walker/Kudos Editorial and Design Services

First American publication 1993 by New Discovery Books, Macmillan Publishing Company, 866 Third Avenue, New York, NY 10022

Macmillan Publishing Company is part of the Maxwell Communication Group of Companies.

First Published in 1992 by Wayland (Publishers) Ltd
61 Western Road, Hove, East Sussex BN3 1JD

Printed in Italy by G. Canale & C.S.p.A., Turin

10 9 8 7 6 5 4 3 2 1

Library of Congress Cataloging-in-Publication Data

Harbor, Bernard.
    The breakup of the Soviet Union/ Bernard Harbor.
       p.   cm. — (Conflicts)
    Summary: Examines the breakdown of communism in the Soviet Union, with examples of what life was like before 1917 and how things have been since the dissolution of the Soviet.
    ISBN 0-02-742625-4
    1. Soviet Union—Politics and government—1985-1991—Juvenile literature.
[1.Soviet Union—Politics and government—1985-1991.] I Title. II. Series: Conflicts
DK288.H36 1993
947.08'8—dc20
                                          92-19917

Contents

CHAPTER 1

CONFLICT IN THE SOVIET UNION

Conflict takes many forms. Usually we associate it with the fighting and wars that we see on television or read about in the newspapers. But fighting is only one kind of conflict. Conflict can arise between people who hold different political opinions or have different ethnic backgrounds. It also comes from tensions caused by economic problems, when people do not have the things they need or want.

Conflicts can occur between individuals, between the people of a country and its government, or between separate nations and states. There may not be obvious signs, such as demonstrations, revolution, or war, but a lack of violent action does not always mean that people have no grievances.

Although in the Soviet Union the threat or possibility of physical conflict was ever present, this book shows how conflicts there took many forms. And, although violence broke out on many occasions, the conflicts that arose from the political and economic changes brought about during the leadership of President Mikhail Gorbachev were relatively free from physical violence.

The conflicts in the Soviet Union became so great that in 1991 it finally broke apart and was replaced by a new system of government—the Commonwealth of Independent States. In order to understand why that happened, it is important to look back at the Soviet Union, especially the Gorbachev years, from 1985 to 1991.

In this book, the causes of conflict leading to the breakup of the Union have been separated into chapters—relating, for example, to economic,

President Brezhnev (fifth from the right) *reviews the May Day parade in Moscow in 1978.*

After the attempted coup in August 1991, a soldier waves a flag from which the hammer and sickle, emblem of the Communist Party, has been cut out.

political, or nationalist issues. But it is important to bear in mind that these separate issues are connected. Economic problems affect political decisions. The requirements of the army can affect the economy. And the history and geography of nations influence the views, concerns, and demands of their peoples and the possibilities for resolving conflicts.

The story of the last years of the Soviet Union is an exciting one. Seldom has history shown such massive changes over such a short period of time. In 1985, the year when Mikhail Gorbachev became the country's leader, the Soviet Union was a closed society ruled exclusively by the Communist Party. Just six years later, the Communist Party had been swept from political

life in the country, and Gorbachev was president of a Union that no longer existed.

For years the Soviet Union was seen as a huge and unchanging state, and its relationships with other countries, in the West, in Eastern Europe, and in the developing world, were stable. But from the mid-1980s this situation changed at great and increasing speed. This makes the story of change in the Soviet Union interesting in itself, but it also tells us a lot about how different forms of conflict can occur and about the dangers and opportunities of rapid political change. It also gives us a chance to look at the merits and problems of one of the greatest conflicts of the 20th century—between the political and economic creeds of capitalism and communism.

1917–1945: WAR AND FAMINE

There have been three great turning points in Soviet history: the Bolshevik revolution of 1917, which established the Soviet Union as a Communist state; World War II, when the country suffered devastating attacks from Nazi Germany; and the period of Mikhail Gorbachev's leadership, beginning in 1985, which is the main subject of this book. Each of these periods is associated with one of the three towering figures of Soviet history: the first with Vladimir Ilyich Lenin, the great revolutionary and political thinker; the second with Lenin's successor, Joseph Stalin; and the third with Gorbachev himself.

T he Soviet Union was born in conflict and throughout its short history its people experienced attack from outside and a continual struggle to survive within the Soviet state. It is impossible to understand the conflicts of the 1980s and 1990s without knowing something of the country's history.

Prerevolutionary Russia

Before the 1917 revolution the Russian empire had been ruled by autocratic czars for over 300 years. A czar was an emperor who had absolute control over all aspects of the state, its

Lenin (left) and Stalin, the leaders whose influence on Soviet politics and economics lasted right up to the Gorbachev years.

Russian workers in a factory canteen in 1904. Many hoped that the Bolshevik revolution of 1917 would put an end to scenes like this.

government, and its armed forces. Russian society was extremely unequal. The czar and the aristocracy lived in the wealth and splendor of any European elite, but most of the people lived in terrible poverty. In the first half of the nineteenth century, most country dwellers were serfs—literally slaves who were owned by their landlords just as if they were farm animals. The system of serfdom was abolished in 1861, because it was felt that it held back the development of a modern agricultural and industrial system. But for most people who lived and worked in the country, life remained hard. They were paid as laborers but had to work long hours for low

wages and they experienced periods of unemployment at certain times of year. For all country dwellers, but especially the sick and elderly, hunger and even starvation were common.

In the cities, conditions were different but not much better. Russia was slow to develop its industry compared with other world powers like Britain, Germany, and the United States, but the abolition of serfdom in 1861 meant that thousands of peasants flocked to the cities where industry was growing. Here employment was more regular, but conditions and wages were still very bad. There was no welfare system.

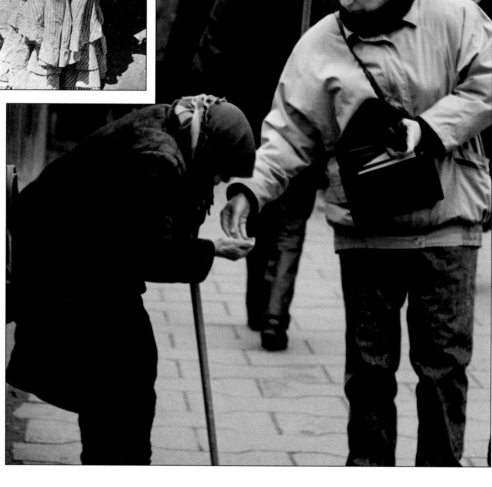

Under the czars, many Russian people faced poverty when old or sick (inset). *In the late 1980s, worsening economic conditions again forced people to beg on the streets.*

Unless their families could take care of them, sick and elderly people could only turn to begging. There was no state education.

The army ruled over Russia's colonies in a ruthless manner, brutally suppressing the native peoples. But even within the Russian army inequality was the rule. Living conditions for ordinary soldiers were worse than for factory workers. As well, discipline was harsh. Soldiers could be flogged or beaten almost to death for the most minor breaches of discipline.

The Bolshevik revolution

The conditions of poverty and oppression in the country led many political groups to demand far-reaching reforms in the early 1900s. But it was the Bolshevik group of revolutionaries that eventually seized power when discontent boiled over. The Bolsheviks were Marxists who believed that a small revolutionary elite would lead workers and peasants to overthrow the czars and establish a socialist state. They formed the Communist Party in the Soviet Union.

The Bolsheviks were strong in the cities, especially St. Petersburg (which was later renamed Leningrad after the Bolshevik leader). Their rallying cry of "Peace, bread, and land" was intended to appeal to soldiers, workers, and peasants.

During 1917 there were two revolutions. The first, in February, removed the czar from power and replaced him with an interim government. The second, in October, saw the Bolsheviks seize power from the interim government. This was made possible when the terrible conditions suffered by Russian soldiers fighting in World War I (1914-1918) led many to rebel against their officers and desert the army to join the revolutionary cause.

The years after the revolution

The revolution itself was not particularly violent. Its most famous act, the storming of the Winter Palace in St. Petersburg, where members of the government were arrested by the revolutionaries, left fewer casualties than occurred in the reconstruction of the event in 1928 by the famous Soviet filmmaker Sergei Eisenstein for his film *October*. But the years immediately following the revolution saw the new Soviet state fighting a civil war against the White Guards (Russians who wanted a return to the czarist system) and

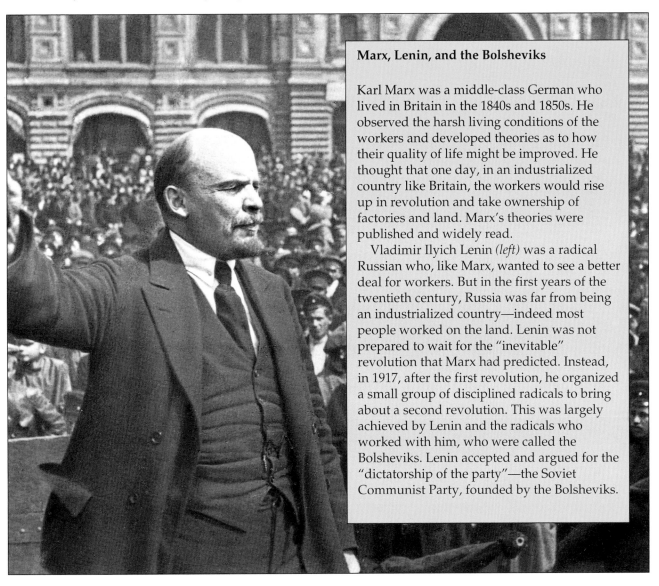

Marx, Lenin, and the Bolsheviks

Karl Marx was a middle-class German who lived in Britain in the 1840s and 1850s. He observed the harsh living conditions of the workers and developed theories as to how their quality of life might be improved. He thought that one day, in an industrialized country like Britain, the workers would rise up in revolution and take ownership of factories and land. Marx's theories were published and widely read.

Vladimir Ilyich Lenin *(left)* was a radical Russian who, like Marx, wanted to see a better deal for workers. But in the first years of the twentieth century, Russia was far from being an industrialized country—indeed most people worked on the land. Lenin was not prepared to wait for the "inevitable" revolution that Marx had predicted. Instead, in 1917, after the first revolution, he organized a small group of disciplined radicals to bring about a second revolution. This was largely achieved by Lenin and the radicals who worked with him, who were called the Bolsheviks. Lenin accepted and argued for the "dictatorship of the party"—the Soviet Communist Party, founded by the Bolsheviks.

This picture, taken in 1936, shows a positive image of work on a collective farm —showing a state-provided machine at work. But reality was different, as millions died during the famines of the 1930s.

against invasion forces from the Western powers who were determined that the new Communist state would not last. Leon Trotsky, the second most powerful person in Lenin's government, organized the revolutionary forces into the Red Army, which defeated the White Guards and pushed back the foreign invaders.

At the time of the revolution, Lenin had said that it would not succeed unless there was also revolution in one or more of the other major industrialized countries. However, as it soon became obvious this was not going to happen, the Soviet Union found that it was therefore necessary to create "socialism in one country." Among other things, this meant that a large and modern army became a permanent feature of the new Communist state (the effects of this are discussed in chapter 7).

Between the wars

Lenin died in 1924 and was replaced by Joseph Stalin. Stalin believed that in order to survive, the Soviet Union had to modernize its economy and agriculture—to catch up with and overtake the capitalist countries. He set about the rapid industrialization of the economy, to improve the efficiency of industry and agriculture. This was to be done through central planning, with a series of "five-year plans" creating targets for industrial and agricultural output.

In the rural areas, Stalin introduced a policy of gathering agricultural activity into large collective farms and began to introduce modern machinery. But the collectivization program failed to meet the government's expectations, and millions of peasants died in the 1930s as famine spread across the countryside.

The main political feature of Stalin's rule was the centralization of state power and ruthless suppression of any disagreement with government policies. In 1929 Trotsky was exiled by Stalin for disagreeing with his policies. (Trotsky was assassinated in 1940 by Stalin's supporters.) This was followed in the 1930s by great show trials of leading political dissenters, which led to their execution or imprisonment.

World War II

Although a nonaggression pact had been signed between Nazi Germany and the Soviet Union, the German army invaded Soviet territory in 1941. Partly because Stalin had purged his own army of most of its leaders in the 1930s, the Soviet Union was unable at first to halt the German invasion. The Nazis reached the outskirts of the capital, Moscow, within five months. About 40 percent of the Soviet population, 40 percent of grain production, and 60 percent of coal, iron, and steel output were captured by the German invasion force. More than one million Soviet soldiers were killed or taken prisoner.

Although they eventually forced the German army to leave, the Soviet people suffered terrible hardships in the war. More than twenty million died, which was about a fifth of the Soviet population and more than the total number of dead from all the other countries at war put together. This great national tragedy also showed the heroism of the people. The 900-day siege of Leningrad and the battle of Stalingrad became symbols of their strength and determination.

The story of the Soviet Union from World War II until 1985 was largely one of slow economic development, huge military expenditure, and political stagnation—with the Communist Party stifling any opposition. The story since 1945 is taken up in chapters 4 to 9.

No country suffered as much as the Soviet Union during World War II. This picture shows a Soviet infantry advance with a T34 tank in 1943 in harsh, wintry conditions.

THE PEOPLES AND PLACES OF THE UNION

The empire that became the Soviet Union following the Bolshevik revolution was the largest single nation on earth. Under the most prominent Russian leaders, Ivan the Terrible (1530-1584), Peter the Great (1672-1725), Catherine the Great (1729-1796), and Alexander I (1777-1825), a huge empire had been built up, which was later added to by Stalin. The full extent of the Soviet Union covered almost 8 million square miles, and even in 1991 it still took eight days to cross the country on the Trans-Siberian Railroad.

Not surprisingly, the territories that made up the Soviet Union were very different. Vast frozen wastes in Siberia, sandy deserts in Kazakhstan, subtropical conditions in Georgia, the huge Ukrainian and Russian plains, as well as busy industrial and political centers like Moscow, Leningrad, and Kiev were all among the different aspects of this vast country.

The landmass of the Soviet Union contained vast natural and industrial resources including oil, natural gas, gold, iron, and coal. In the late 1980s the Soviet Union's major exports were oil, iron, and gas, but it also exported industrial goods and grain. All land, natural resources, commerce, communications, and industry were owned and controlled by the state.

Nationality and culture

The peoples of the Soviet Union were as varied as the geography of the country. In 1990, of a population of some 290 million, only about half were ethnic Russians. The rest of the population was made up of over 20 different nationalities, including Ukrainians, Uzbeks, Belorussians, Kazakhs, Tartars, Azerbaijanis, Armenians, and Georgians.

Most of the national peoples of the Soviet Union spoke their own languages. While Russian was the official language of the central government and administration, local government institutions were allowed to use their national languages, which could also be the first language taught in schools. Speaking Russian could be a distinct advantage in gaining work and promotion, and many people were bilingual. Radio and television broadcasting in the Soviet Union catered to about 70 different languages.

About two-thirds of the population were living in towns and cities, and this number grew as people moved to the urban areas and as the countryside itself became increasingly urbanized. The remaining third of the population lived in the rural areas. About two-thirds of the people worked in industry or state-owned agriculture. The state provided facilities for education and recreation, such as libraries, sports centers, and "parks of culture." In some regions, the people kept certain aspects of local culture, such as particular styles of dress, traditional pastimes, and local festivals—one way in which a sense of national identity could be retained.

Official arts in the Soviet Union—painting and sculpture, literature, and theater—were expected to promote Communist principles and glorify the revolution. Typical examples were seen in the many huge murals and sculptures in public places, portraying Marx, Lenin, and other important Communist figures, and celebrating Soviet achievements. Works that were thought to be critical of approved principles were banned, and writers and artists could be exiled or imprisoned for promoting ideas found unacceptable to the state.

Even in remote rural areas, posters like this one of Lenin reminded the Soviet people of the state's control over their lives.

Another area of potential conflict between the central Soviet government and the diverse peoples of the Union was the discouragement of formal acts of worship and outward displays of religious beliefs. Under the czars, the official religion of the Russian empire had been the Russian Orthodox Church. After the revolution, the Church lost its legal status, and Church property was taken over by the state. Although the individual's right to freedom of religious thought was upheld by the constitution of the Soviet Union, in practice this was not encouraged because a strong belief in God and in a religion's spiritual values was thought to weaken the peoples' allegiance to the Communist state and the principles of Marxist doctrine that it upheld.

Because the Soviet population included so many different nationalities, it also encompassed a variety of religious faiths. As well as Russian Orthodox Christians, there were Protestant and Roman Catholic groups, Jews, Muslims, and Buddhists. Jews and Muslims, particularly, suffered persecution and discrimination at certain times in Soviet history, while Christians often had to suppress their beliefs or worship secretly. A more open attitude toward religion was introduced in the mid-1980s under President Gorbachev's *glasnost* program (see chapter 6), which also took a much more liberal attitude toward the arts.

Although the Soviet Union was officially an atheist (non-religious) state, Communist rule failed to wipe out religious beliefs. In this picture, taken in 1988, the most senior patriarch of the Russian Orthodox Church conducts a service in an act of defiance against atheism. Notice the TV cameras on the left recording the event.

Soviet republics

The Soviet Union was made up of fifteen republics. Each republic took its name from its main nationality, but minorities from other ethnic and national backgrounds also lived there. The republics were themselves divided into some 120 territories, subdivided again into districts, cities, and towns. Chapter 8 discusses the relationship between the republics and the central Soviet government and the growing autonomy of the republics.

Russia dominated the Soviet Union politically, despite making up only half of its population. It was by far the largest republic— over 6.5 million square miles, spanning 11 time zones from Finland to Alaska, and over 2,000 miles from China to the Arctic Ocean. With a population of nearly 150 million, it accounted for 70 percent of Soviet industry and agriculture. Russians dominated the political, industrial, and economic institutions of the Soviet Union.

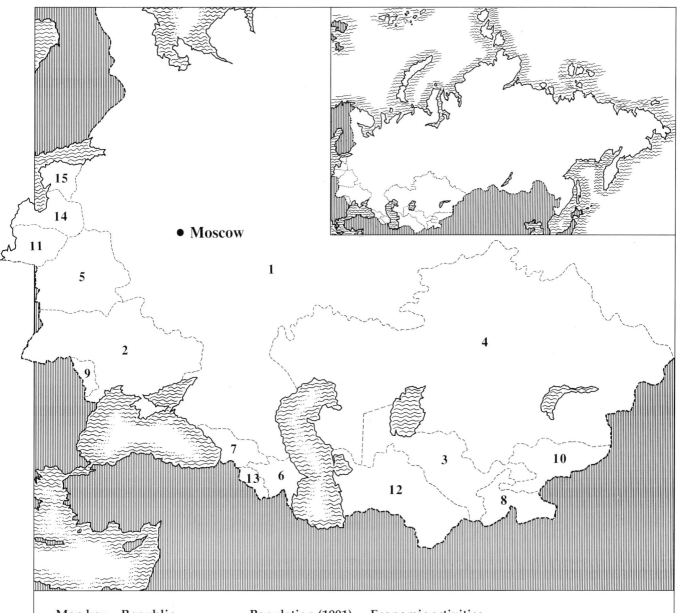

Moscow

Map key	Republic	Population (1991)	Economic activities
1	Russian Federation	148 million	Oil, gold, gas, industrial goods
2	Ukraine	52 million	Steel, iron, coal, foodstuffs, machine tools
3	Uzbekistan	20 million	Cotton, gas
4	Kazakhstan	17 million	Coal, iron, steel
5	Belorussia	10 million	Agricultural equipment, televisions
6	Azerbaijan	7 million	Oil, gas, chemicals
7	Georgia	5 million	Wine, foodstuffs, vehicles
8	Tadzhikistan	5 million	Gold, carpets, textiles, foodstuffs
9	Moldova	4 million	Wine, tobacco, vegetables
10	Kirgizia	4 million	Washing machines, textiles
11	Lithuania	3.7 million	Electrical and electronic goods, motor components
12	Turkmenistan	3.5 million	Gas, salt
13	Armenia	3.3 million	Chemicals, heavy machinery, textiles
14	Latvia	2.7 million	Electronic goods, telecommunications
15	Estonia	1.6 million	Electronics, electric motors, shoes, fish, paper

THE SOVIET ECONOMY

The incredible changes that took place in the Soviet Union in the 1980s and 1990s would not have happened had it not been for the rapid deterioration of the economy. The need to improve economic performance, and the conflicts that arose from poor economic management, led to wide-ranging changes in the economy and politics.

In economic terms, Communist countries have had two distinctive features. First, there was no private property. Apart from personal possessions, everything was owned by the state or other institutions, like the Communist Party. All the factories, farms, stores, means of transportation, and houses were state owned.

Second, while capitalist countries relied on markets to set prices for exchange of goods and services, Communist countries did this through central planning. The government decided what goods and services needed to be produced. It allocated raw materials and capital goods to factories and farms, which were then expected to produce a certain amount of food, goods, or services. These in turn were distributed to stores in the cities and towns, again through central planning.

Economic stagnation

From the time of the Bolshevik revolution, control over property and the economy in the Soviet Union was held by the government. In theory, the government guaranteed low prices, welfare benefits, housing, and jobs for all. Even at the time of the revolution, when hopes were high, meeting these commitments was a formidable challenge. Although the Soviet Union had lots of natural resources and lots of people, which together should have made it possible to produce everything the country needed, industry and agriculture were very backward, especially compared to Britain, Germany, and the United States.

This store sold produce from a Latvian collective farm. Official state prices were kept low; in the Gorbachev era, privatized distribution meant ordinary vegetables could cost up to twenty times the state price.

As standing in line became a way of life, people might wait hours just to obtain basic foods—such as bread.

After the revolution, the new government hoped to do away with the worst poverty by redistributing wealth. It also wanted to increase the total wealth of the country by better planning and organization of the economy, and by modernizing agriculture and industry. But despite the rapid industrialization program and ambitious production planning first introduced in the 1920s and 1930s, by the 1980s it was clear to most observers that the economy was still hopelessly backward.

The Soviet economy suffered from external interference in the years after the revolution. Countries such as Britain and the United States secretly aided the anti-Bolshevik White Guards, sending money and weapons and blocking trade. Then, during the World War II, the German invasion destroyed much of Soviet industry and killed more than 20 million of the country's people. However, the Soviet planning system was rigid and bureaucratic and had itself failed. Production targets had led to an emphasis on the total amount produced rather than the quality of what was produced. State control of the allocation of resources meant that industry was unaware of real costs, and as a result little effort was made to prevent waste and inefficiency. Soviet goods were expensive and of low quality. Often they were also scarce, as production targets were not met or the state-planned distribution system failed.

The system of taxes and subsidies to industry meant that Soviet industry did not relate to world prices. For the most part, the Soviet economy remained outside the world trade system, unable to sell its goods abroad and struggling to pay for its imports.

On top of all this, the attempt to build up bigger armed forces and more nuclear weapons than the United States and NATO used a huge amount of resources. It has been estimated that at least 11 to 12 percent of national wealth was spent on the military. The military buildup, or the arms race, meant that resources could not be spent on improving industry and agriculture or putting more goods in the stores.

By the time Mikhail Gorbachev came to power in 1985 the Soviet Union owed $30 billion to Western countries, a debt that was expected to have grown six times larger by the year 2000. Most farms were bankrupt. Industry was inefficient, unable to deliver the goods at home and incapable of selling them abroad. For the Soviet people this meant a standard of living that was among the lowest in the industrialized world. Many goods, including basic foods,

Chernobyl

Soviet industry was frequently criticized for its devastating impact on the environment. Out-of-date and inefficient factories and mines polluted local environments. But the worst example of environmental damage followed the accident at the nuclear power station in Chernobyl in Belorussia. On April 25, 1986, an unauthorized experiment in the power station went badly wrong, starting a fire in the reactor. The fire burned out of control, releasing huge amounts of highly radioactive material into the atmosphere.

More than twenty-five emergency workers died putting out the fire at Chernobyl. Hundreds of square miles around the power station were evacuated as the clean-up operation began. However, the radioactive contamination proved to be on a massive scale, and some areas may remain uninhabitable for decades, possibly longer. It has been estimated that over the next few decades, fallout from Chernobyl will result in 10,000 to 50,000 additional deaths from cancer across Europe. Chernobyl proved that modernization of Soviet industry was essential to prevent further harm to the environment.

A black marketeer sells jeans, once a much-coveted item of Western-style dress, inside a Moscow department store.

were increasingly hard to find. Housing was scarce and of poor quality. And all the time, the Soviet government was spending more and more money to support industry and agriculture, to pay for imports and to maintain welfare programs.

Perestroika

In the mid-1980s, Soviet leader Mikhail Gorbachev set about reforming the economy under his *perestroika* program. By *perestroika* he meant a fundamental restructuring of the Soviet economy. Initially, his idea was not to replace the communist system of state ownership and central planning, but to discipline it, improve and modernize it.

His ambitious aim was to double the amount of goods and services produced within fifteen years and to bring their quality up to Western standards. To achieve this, radical measures were announced. Factories that regularly lost money were allowed to go bankrupt. Food subsidies were reduced. Farmers were allowed to lease land from the state and thus make a private profit from their work. Limited private enterprise was allowed, and the state cut its spending drastically.

Radical though it was, *perestroika* could not overcome the sluggishness in the Soviet economy. It failed to introduce systems that could balance the supply of food and goods with people's demand for them. In capitalist countries, price is theoretically controlled by supply and demand in the free market. But the only Soviet market that emerged was the black market, selling scarce goods at high prices. A few people became much richer on the black market and through small private enterprises, but for most people the economic situation merely deteriorated.

In the late 1980s, both output from factories and exports continued to fall. The government continued to spend more in subsidies and welfare than it received in taxes from its ailing industry

—its budget deficit grew five times larger as a proportion of national wealth in the first three years of *perestroika* (1985 to 1988). More imports were needed, but the Soviet Union was less and less able to pay. In the first two years of *perestroika*, economic growth actually declined. The transportation system deteriorated and military spending continued to drain resources.

While his political critics called for privatization (where state-owned companies and institutions are sold off to private buyers) and the end of controls on prices and wages, Gorbachev continued with his gradual reforms. He moved away from state planning, allowing firms to negotiate between themselves. A few joint ventures with Western companies and cooperatives were set up. But, again, these changes were not enough to stop the decline, and as basic goods and foods became more scarce, opposition to Gorbachev grew. Panic-buying of almost any foods and goods became common in the big cities.

By the time price controls were lifted in 1991 Gorbachev had become the major focus of discontent. In the spring of 1990, thousands of miners across the country went on strike, calling for him to resign, and he was forced to leave the traditional May Day parade in Moscow because of a massive demonstration against him.

With the economy in a desperate mess,

> **Inefficiency in the Soviet Union**
>
> The centrally planned economy was inefficient for a number of reasons. These included:
> ☆ Central decision-making meant little incentive for local factories to make improvements.
> ☆ Agriculture, factories, and producers of raw materials were located thousands of miles apart, leading to wasteful transportation of materials and goods among them.
> ☆ Scarce resources were channeled into military production.
> ☆ The prices of raw materials, the Soviet Union's main exports, fell on international markets.
> ☆ As a result of industrial and agricultural inefficiency, the price of food rose much faster than wages.

Gorbachev attempted to plot a gradual course between the old ways of central planning and the free market (being demanded by reformers in the Soviet Union and by politicians in the West). The failed coup on August 19, 1991, intended to remove Gorbachev from power, was an attempt by the old guard to draw back from *perestroika*. With the failure of the coup, the Soviet economy was set to change much more rapidly and much more drastically than Gorbachev had imagined.

Although miners were among the highest-paid Soviet workers, the appalling conditions in which they lived and worked led thousands to strike in 1990, demanding a better deal. These men are from Prokopyevsk in the Kuznetsk region. The miners' strike almost brought down Gorbachev's government.

DAILY LIFE

The economic problems in the Soviet Union are not just a question of figures and policies; they have a very real impact on people's day-to-day lives. In the early years after the Bolshevik revolution, people could compare their economic circumstances with the poverty of life under the czar. The promise of a better future meant that people were prepared to put up with economic hardships.

However, in later years modern communications have enabled the Soviet people to compare their lot with conditions in other countries. While the government was able to guarantee jobs, stable prices, and welfare benefits, the people accepted what was a lower standard of living than in most industrialized countries. But as expectations of a better life grew with Gorbachev's *perestroika* policies, the economic situation deteriorated. People became more and more discontent with their situation, and this led them to challenge the Soviet system and demand more far-reaching changes.

Life in the Soviet Union
In chapter 2 we got a glimpse of the wide range of different places and peoples in the vast Soviet state. There were many different ways of life and experiences in the country, but the economic

Pickling vegetables for winter in the kitchen of a cooperative farm in Lithuania.

Moscow teenagers. Compared to the Cold War years, youth culture flourished in the late 1980s. There were tours from Western pop groups, and the latest fashions were always available through the black market.

problems meant that few people could live very comfortably. Most city dwellers occupy apartments where conditions are cramped and drab. While luxury goods, especially those imported from other countries, have always been scarce and expensive, basic foods have been cheap and easily available in the towns, and especially in the countryside where they were produced. But toward the end of the 1980s, it became more difficult to find food, and standing in line became a way of life. Of course, lines are a common sight in many countries, but in Soviet cities people often have to stand in them for long periods of time, perhaps two or three hours, to buy even the most basic foods.

With meat, cheese, and eggs very scarce, city dwellers spend many hours a day searching for food and other necessities. In 1990 the citizens of Moscow panicked when for a few days even bread was impossible to find. People feared that famine was on the way and began to buy any food they could get, to store at home. After that, empty stores became a common sight and people would regularly drop into these stores just on the chance of finding something they needed. The slightest rumor of new stock was enough for people to start forming lines.

A number of measures were taken in 1991 to deal with the food crisis. In Moscow, it was no longer possible to buy food without giving proof of permanent residence in the city. This was to prevent outsiders from coming into the city to stock up. In Leningrad, the country's second largest city, food rationing was introduced. In the meantime the government attempted to secure loans of money and food from other countries. But while the Soviet people spent hour in line, they were not able to produce the goods to pay for these and other imports.

Until *perestroika*, paying for food was not such a problem, for prices were controlled by the government. Its attempts to reduce price controls to encourage more production led to fears that, although more food might be available, it would be too expensive for many families. It was already possible to buy food on the black market, but with prices at up to ten times more than store prices, this was way beyond the means of ordinary Soviet families.

Discontent and protest

Like all modern societies, the Soviet Union witnessed discontent from its people. However, before Gorbachev, the Soviet people were not able to protest openly, and they suffered particular hardships. Because of this their discontent was expressed in other ways. Social problems like alcoholism became widespread.

By Moscow standards, where living space per person was officially restricted, this apartment kitchen is fairly large. The family probably spent many hours standing in lines to be able to enjoy this simple meal.

McDonald's in Moscow brought an example of capitalism to the heart of the Communist state, but prices in the Soviet Union were unrealistic by Western standards. One dollar would buy 24 gallons of gasoline or food for a Soviet family for one week.

A grim Soviet sense of humor often carried the people through.

As the economy worsened, protests became more serious. In 1991, miners from the Ukraine and Kazakhstan went on strike, as did 80,000 industrial workers in Belorussia. Miners were among the highest paid workers in the country and their demands did not include higher wages. Rather they wanted better working and environmental conditions and to be supplied with basic commodities like soap.

Down with *perestroika*!

The day-to-day struggle of life in the country was frustrating and wasteful. While people were standing in line they could not produce goods, but they did have time to think about and discuss their predicament and to think of alternative ways of life. For many, the promise of Western-style economics seemed more and more attractive. For others, even the period of stagnation under former President Brezhnev became a fond memory: life had not been easy then, but at least they had jobs, and food was readily available. Either way, no one seemed to benefit from *perestroika*.

Soviet humor

A Moscow woman had stood in line for three hours for meat. In all that time the line had not moved.

"That's it!" she said. "I've had enough of this. I'm going to assassinate President Gorbachev." With this she stormed off, only to return an hour later.

"What happened?" asked her friends. "Did you assassinate the president?"

"I didn't have time," she replied. "The line was too long."

POLITICS, GORBACHEV, AND *GLASNOST*

Before Mikhail Gorbachev came to power, the Communist Party was all-powerful in Soviet politics and its influence over Soviet society was total. All other political parties were illegal and any debate about different policies happened only within the Party. Open criticism of the Party or the Soviet system by individuals or in the media was punished by imprisonment or exile. The leader of the Party was automatically the leader of the country. The ruling committee of the Party (the Politburo) effectively ran the government. All leading positions in government departments, industry, the media, and the armed forces, even the arts and sciences, were filled by Party members. In almost any area, it was necessary to be a Party member in order to have a successful career.

Most of the people who held the important positions in the Communist Party were very suspicious of change. From the time of Stalin only the most gradual change occurred. The country's leaders were appointed from within the Party. For example, Nikita Khrushchev (appointed as leader in 1958) was quickly replaced (in 1964) once he started on a course of rapid reform.

However, even when Gorbachev was appointed leader in 1985, it was known that he wanted reform. At the age of fifty-four he was young for the job and he was soon to prove himself different from past leaders. Within two days of becoming Party leader he announced plans to reform the economy—the *perestroika* program described in chapter 4. In the following years his reforms went much further than even the most liberal Party member could have imagined in 1985; but until 1991, Gorbachev attempted to balance demands for political and economic reforms with the conservative ideas of the "old guard" in the Party establishment.

Glasnost and *demokratizatsiya*

Hand in hand with his economic policy of *perestroika*, Gorbachev introduced sweeping political reforms, which he termed *glasnost*, translated as "openness," and *demokratizatsiya* or "democratization." Gorbachev's reforms allowed people to criticize the Communist Party and even himself.

One of the first people to benefit from *glasnost* was Andrei Sakharov, a scientist who had criticized President Brezhnev back in 1966. He had been exiled to the city of Gorky (closed to foreigners and visitors) since 1968. In 1986 Gorbachev allowed the dissident scientist to return from exile. Sakharov later became a representative in the Soviet Parliament.

Less than two years after the *perestroika* program had begun, economic reforms had already run into difficulties. Gorbachev said that political reforms were necessary for economic reforms to succeed. In 1987 he began the process

---

The media and *glasnost*

Glasnost brought a whole crop of newspapers, magazines, books, and plays to the Soviet public. Examples of proreform publications that came with *glasnost* were the newspaper *Moscow News* and *Ogonyuk* —a popular current affairs magazine. The circulation of *Ogonyuk* rose from 300,000, when it started in 1986, to over three million in 1990.

Posters of the Communist heroes, like this one of Lenin, were a common sight in cities and towns until the 1990s.

of democratization by introducing the right for Communist Party members to elect Party officials, rather than have them appointed by senior Party members.

When, the following year, Gorbachev saw that there was still resistance to change at all levels of the Party, he began to shift power away from it. The first genuine elections to government bodies in which the people could choose between Party members and nonmembers occurred in 1989. Elections took place for the soviets (councils) in each of the republics and for the Supreme Soviet, which governed the whole country. For the first time there was opposition within the soviets.

In the meantime, Communist reformers were gradually replacing the conservatives within the Party. Dissent was also allowed in the media, which began to criticize government policy and discuss alternatives. But as the reforms became

Andrei Sakharov, one-time nuclear weapons scientist, became Russia's leading dissident.

The Supreme Soviet: under Gorbachev, the Soviet Union's political system became more like parliamentary systems in the West.

more far reaching and more and more discussion took place, demands grew for even wider and more radical change. In 1990, 200,000 people marched to the Kremlin demanding an end to the Communist Party's official monopoly of power. Gorbachev soon gave in to this and other demands and the Party's leading role was abolished. Thereafter its official status was no different from that of any other political party.

By this time the revolution that had been begun by Gorbachev from above was being taken over from below. Boris Yeltsin, previously thrown out of the government by Gorbachev, had become

The old Soviet system of government

Before the rapid changes that followed the coup of August 1991, Soviet government was based on three main bodies:

The Congress of People's Deputies

The Congress of People's Deputies was the highest state authority and was responsible for formulating and amending the constitution and for laying down guidelines for the general thrust of domestic and foreign policy.

It was made up of 2,250 delegates: 1,500 represented various territories and national districts while the other 750 represented "public organizations" including the Communist Party and the trade unions.

In 1989, 88 percent of People's Deputies were Communist Party members. The president of the Soviet Union was elected by the Congress of People's Deputies, which also endorsed the Council of Ministers, and the Congress was responsible for electing the Supreme Soviet of the Soviet Union.

The Supreme Soviet

The Supreme Soviet was the permanent law-making body of the Soviet Union and dealt with detailed policy questions on all issues that affected the Soviet Union as a whole. These included defense and internal state security, foreign policy and diplomacy, setting the budget, economic planning, foreign trade, and education.

The Supreme Soviets of the Union republics

All matters relating to government of republics that were not carried out by the Supreme Soviet were the responsibility of the Supreme Soviets of the Union republics. Similar soviets also existed for the "autonomous districts," which were regional subdivisions of the republics.

Local government

The Soviet Union was divided into 15 republics, which, in turn, were divided into 120 territories and regions with over 3,000 districts, including the autonomous districts.

At all levels government was undertaken by soviets (or councils) whose deputies (or representatives) were elected. Everyone over the age of eighteen was eligible to vote.

the focus of the movement for reform. In 1991, Yeltsin was elected president of the Russian Federation. Gorbachev became less and less popular at home. The leader who had once walked freely around Soviet cities talking to the people now had 200 official bodyguards.

Calls grew for more political and economic power to be moved away from the Supreme Soviet to the republics. In February 1991, as prices rose and goods became more scarce, Gorbachev's resignation was demanded by Boris Yeltsin, striking miners, and Moscow demonstrators.

Gorbachev's balancing act

Gorbachev had to balance the desire for reform against the power of the hard-liners in the Party. Although the Party was in decline, until the middle of 1991 the hard-liners still had control of the security forces—the army, the police, and the KGB (the secret service). If reform went too far too quickly, Gorbachev feared that the hard-liners would seize power and put a stop to the process altogether.

Gorbachev was also concerned that if too much power was given to the republics, the Soviet Union would fall apart. Instead of being a superpower, the Union would divide into a number of smaller, chaotic, and less powerful nations. Although he wanted political reform, he saw the Communist Party as the only organization capable of keeping the country together and chaos at bay.

Up until June/July 1991 Gorbachev attempted to travel the middle way between the Communist conservatives and the radical reformers. He then began to show more sympathy toward Yeltsin and the radicals. Eventually he told Communist Party members that the Party must "reform or die." It must abandon the communist ideology and embrace the idea of a society with private property and a welfare system.

Despite its grip on the security forces, the Communist Party's influence in Soviet society had declined rapidly since the mid-1980s. In elections it had lost control in the three major Soviet cities—Moscow, Leningrad, and Kiev— and in hundreds of other towns and cities. By the beginning of 1991, most of the republics had non-Communist majorities in their parliaments and many were seeking more and more independence from the central Soviet government. In the eighteen months leading up to the attempted coup of August 1991, nearly 5 million members had left the Party.

In the six years between 1985 and 1991, power had shifted from the Party to the Soviet Parliament, and the government had become subordinate to the Parliament. The last bastion of Communist Party influence was the armed forces, which were to play a decisive role in the attempted coup, an event bringing fatal consequences for the once all-powerful Party.

Boris Yeltsin is pictured here in front of the statue of Lenin in the Supreme Soviet; after the events of the 1991 coup, he would encourage the Russians to remove such symbols of the Communist Party.

THE MILITARY MACHINE

Throughout its history, and especially after World War II, the armed forces in the Soviet Union had a central influence in political and economic policy, as well as military strategy. The military was influential in domestic policy as well as Soviet foreign policy.

Soviet military power—symbolized by missiles like these —was demonstrated annually at the May Day parade in Moscow (seen here in 1961).

At the time of the 1917 revolution, the rebellion among the ordinary soldiers was a key element in the success of the Bolsheviks. But Lenin believed that in the socialist state, there would be no need for a standing army. Rather, the workers and peasants would rally to defend the revolution as necessary. But during the civil war with the White Guards, Lenin was to call for an army of first one and then three million soldiers to defend the Soviet state. Later, when the Soviet Union was forced to follow the policy of "socialism in one country," it became obvious that the Soviet Union would need military power to defend itself against external threats.

In the years immediately following the revolution, Trotsky organized the Red Army with strict discipline and centralized control against criticism from within the Party. In the mid-1920s, under Stalin's leadership, a strong and modern standing army became central to defense policy. Furthermore, in line with the aim of catching up with and surpassing the capitalist powers, the Soviet Union was determined to equip its armed forces with the most modern and effective military technology.

The size and strength of Soviet armed forces

Following World War II, the superpower status of the Soviet Union rested upon its massive armed forces. The only other country with comparable military strength was the world's other superpower, the United States.

In 1991:
- ✯ The Soviet Army had 1.5 million soldiers, of whom 1.2 million were conscripts. An additional 437,000 sailors and 448,000 air force personnel made up the bulk of the armed services.
- ✯ The Soviet nuclear weapons force included 1,450 intercontinental ballistic missiles, over 600 nuclear bomber aircraft, and 64 strategic submarines. Only the United States could match this nuclear force.
- ✯ Conventional forces included over 40,000 tanks, 6,000 fighter aircraft , and nearly 500 naval vessels.

Soviet soldiers had to take on many civilian jobs, helping to keep up essential services and supplies. Here they are working on the potato harvest.

One of the key aims of Stalin's policy of rapid industrialization, then, was to equip the army with the best weapons that technology could offer and make the Soviet Union a leading military power. Before long, the armed forces were a priority area with privileged access to economic and technological resources. The aim of developing and then keeping strong armed forces soon became the most important Soviet industrial policy.

The Warsaw Pact

The Soviet Union led the Warsaw Pact from 1955 until the dissolution of the pact in 1990. The pact was an organization for mutual defense consisting of all the Eastern European countries —Bulgaria, Czechoslovakia, East Germany, Hungary, Poland, and Romania. Although the Warsaw Pact had more personnel and conventional equipment than its Western counterpart, NATO, it was argued that because its organization and equipment were inferior,

there was a rough balance of military force between East and West.

Despite the end of the Cold War between the superpowers, the legacy of Soviet military power remained. The Soviet Union was spending between 15 and 25 percent of its national wealth on defense. But some estimates say that military production accounted for over 60 percent of all the goods manufactured in the Soviet Union. Therefore, one of its main economic challenges was to "convert" its military production to civil production.

The nuclear arms race

After World War II the military effort was redoubled. The Soviets were shocked at the ease with which the German army had invaded, and the consequences were so devastating that they were determined it would never happen again. Equally, the demonstration of America's nuclear power, when atomic bombs were dropped on the Japanese cities of Hiroshima and Nagasaki in

In August 1988 Soviet forces withdrew from Afghanistan after nine years of occupation with reputation and morale badly damaged.

Soviet military intervention since 1945

June 1948   Berlin Blockade: to try to stop Western Allies from reuniting Germany, Soviet army blocks railroads and road routes into West Berlin (then a part of Germany controlled by the United States, Britain, and France). Western countries decide to supply Berlin by air in Berlin Airlift. Airlift continues until May 1949; Soviets back down, agreeing to reopen land routes, but soon afterward Germany is separated into two states: East Germany and West Germany.

October 23, 1956   Soviet tanks sent in to aid Hungarian Communist government in dealing with demonstrations. Soviet troops leave, but return on November 4 when new Hungarian government declares neutrality. Hungarians rebel against Soviet army, but Soviets overwhelm resistance. Some 30,000 Hungarians die in uprising.

August 20, 1968   Soviet and other Warsaw Pact tanks invade Czechoslovakia to force liberal leader Alexander Dubcek to back down on reform plan.

December 27, 1979   Soviet troops enter Afghanistan to support unpopular Communist government.

August 1945, made the Soviets determined to develop their own nuclear forces. They did this very quickly, detonating their own nuclear weapon in 1949. By the mid-1950s they were able to challenge the United States in many areas of nuclear weapons technology.

More and more economic resources were allocated to military programs, whether nuclear or conventional. The annual May Day celebrations in Moscow's Red Square increasingly came to symbolize the military power of the Union. But the image of Soviet military power was not always matched by the reality.

Soviet industry found it harder and harder to keep pace with Western technology. Soviet troops were, for the most part, poorly educated and poorly trained conscripts. With all the different ethnic groups in the Soviet Union, conscripts came from different cultural backgrounds, and ethnic divisions in the armed forces were a serious obstacle to maintaining an effective fighting force. Many Soviet conscripts could not even speak Russian. For some, allegiance to the Soviet Union was not as strong as allegiance to their republic or their religion. Poor conditions in the armed forces undermined their morale and effectiveness even further.

The military and civil society

In daily life, however, the distinction between military and civil society in the Soviet Union was often blurred. Arms-producing factories often also produced civilian goods. Likewise, civilian factories were able to switch to military production if necessary. Conscript soldiers were regularly used to do tasks that, in most industrialized countries, would be done by civilians. These included running transportation services, carrying out construction work, and even helping with agricultural production.

The military chiefs had a powerful influence on Soviet politics. Their links with the Communist Party were very strong. Although most soldiers were conscripts, over 75 percent of the officers were Communist Party members. At the highest ranks, all officers were Party members. Within the armed forces the Party was able to instill rigorous discipline and to educate conscripts in communist beliefs and ideas. As all Soviet men over eighteen were eligible for military service, the entire male population could be made familiar with communist ideas and taught to respect the Party's authority.

From Trotsky onward, military commanders were included at the highest level of government, and here it was almost impossible to separate the military from the Communist Party and the state. The Soviet military interventions in the Eastern European communist states of Hungary (in 1956) and Czechoslovakia (in 1968) served to remind the Soviet people that the military could also be used to put down open rebellion against Communist rule at home.

In the first years after World War II, soldiers were seen as heroes and held in high esteem. But increasingly people began to resent the military's influence at home and their adventures abroad. The long and unsuccessful occupation of Afghanistan (1979 to 1988) led many Soviet women, mothers and wives of conscripts, to campaign openly against the war and against conscription. When under Gorbachev the Soviet army finally withdrew from Afghanistan in defeat, its image was badly tarnished.

After Gorbachev rose to the Soviet leadership and the people's expectations of economic and political reforms grew, the conservative influence of the military on Soviet society was increasingly resented. Furthermore, the Soviet people felt indignant that the armed forces had first claim over industrial resources when ordinary citizens were unable to get the consumer goods enjoyed in other industrialized countries. People felt that the military was resisting change simply to protect its privileged position.

When Soviet troops violently put down demonstrations against the government, killing and injuring the citizens they were supposed to protect (for instance in Uzbekistan in June 1989), any remaining respect or support disappeared. So, when in a last desperate attempt to stop reform, the military and Party leaders attempted a military coup in August 1991, there was no support from the population. Indeed, many soldiers themselves refused to act against the people and, just as in the Bolshevik revolution, some even joined with the protesters to protect the Russian Parliament from attack.

A soldier shakes hands with a demonstrator following the coup of August 1991. The failure of the coup was due to lack of support from the military, who in this case would not act against the Soviet people.

THE GORBACHEV ERA: NEW PROBLEMS

One of the great ironies of the Gorbachev era was that, in order to push through reforms that were unpopular in the political establishment, Gorbachev drew more and more powers to himself. As both leader of the Communist Party and resident of the Soviet Union, he increased the power of both roles, thus increasing his influence in the Party and the Union. Gorbachev, the great reformer, made himself the most powerful Soviet leader since the dictator Stalin.

As criticism was increasingly directed against him, Gorbachev came to symbolize the Union.

January 1990: Gorbachev argues with Lithuanians who were eager to see an independent Lithuania.

With growing demands for political reforms, and a worsening economy, opposition to the Soviet system more frequently took the form of calls for greater independence for the republics. On this issue, Gorbachev was closer to the old guard than on any other. For the reasons outlined in chapter 6, he was determined to keep the Union together, even if this meant a return to repression, at least on some occasions.

Despite the diversity of Soviet history and cultures, the dominance of the Communist Party since the Bolshevik revolution had silenced debate. When political debate surfaced as a result of *glasnost* and *perestroika*, demands for national independence in the republics soon became the strongest form of opposition to the Soviet system. As early as 1988, nationalist groups were calling openly for independence. Each republic had a different history and different demands. But in each case, there were no other well-organized political groups outside the Communist Party, and so the nationalists quickly became the rallying point for opposition to the centralized Soviet government.

In 1988 Armenians rejected Gorbachev's proposals for constitutional change. A long-running dispute between Armenia and Azerbaijan over control of the Nagorno-Karabakh Region boiled over into violent conflict. The following year nationalist demonstrations broke out in Moldova.

In Georgia, 19 people were killed by Soviet soldiers when they clashed with demonstrators in the Georgian city of Tbilisi in April 1989. Scenes of demonstrators being attacked by soldiers armed with tear gas and sharpened spades were shown around the world and around the Soviet Union. This demonstrated the lengths to which the government and military were prepared to go to in order to keep the Union together, if only by force. But the violent deaths of the young demonstrators and the ruthlessness of the state failed to stem the nationalist demands.

Later, in June 1989, over seventy people were killed in demonstrations in Uzbekistan. The Baltic states of Lithuania, Latvia, and Estonia demanded independence, and their representatives walked

Nearly half a million people gathered in Baku, the Azerbaijani capital, for this funeral following ethnic violence in the city in September 1990. The conflict in Azerbaijan was to outlive the Soviet system.

out of the Soviet Congress in protest.

Russians and non-Russians

Ethnic and nationalist groups saw little difference between the Soviet Union and the old Russian empire. As we have seen, for the most part the country inherited by the Bolsheviks was already a vast empire covering many ethnic groups and nationalities. The last countries to be brought under Soviet rule were the Baltic states (Lithuania, Latvia, and Estonia) which were annexed in 1940 following the pact between the Soviet Union and Nazi Germany.

Like all empires, the Russian empire contained many nationalities and ethnic groups. These peoples were divided or grouped together by borders set out by generals and politicians who often had little knowledge of the places they were splitting apart or throwing together. In some cases, as in Moldova, ethnic or national

Nagorno-Karabakh

Nagorno-Karabakh is a small region just inside the republic of Azerbaijan near the Armenian border. Although geographically it is inside Azerbaijan, for centuries most of the people who have lived there have been Armenians. Throughout the twentieth century, the Armenians of Nagorno-Karabakh wanted the region to become part of Armenia. This was fiercely resisted by the Azerbaijanis: Armenians living in Nagorno-Karabakh were not allowed to travel to Armenia and their culture was repressed.

When Gorbachev's *perestroika* program was launched, the Armenians of Nagorno-Karabakh pressed their claims and voted to unite with Armenia. They were supported by the Armenian Republic but provoked a harsh response from the Azerbaijanis. Local Armenian minorities in Azerbaijan were attacked by organized gangs. Furthermore, the Azerbaijanis blockaded Nagorno-Karabakh. From the summer of 1989, Azerbaijan imposed a food and fuel blockade of Armenia itself, which formerly received 85 percent of its supplies via Azerbaijan.

groups were separated by the borders. In others, like Azerbaijan, ethnic minorities found themselves surrounded by hostile majorities. The strength of central Soviet control had kept the lid on regional conflicts throughout most of the twentieth century. But the growing weakness of the central Soviet government in the years leading up to 1991 meant that conflicts between nationalists and the center, and between different ethnic and national groups, became a more and more common feature of Soviet life.

The conflict between the republics and the central government was partly the result of a belief that Russians dominated the empire, as they had done under the czars. In 1991, just over half of the population of the Soviet Union was Russian, leaving some 140 million people belonging to non-Russian ethnic and national groups. For most of these, Soviet rule differed little from the colonial rule of the czars.

These Armenian children in Nagorno-Karabakh went on hunger strike in 1989 to press the case that their region should become part of Armenia.

Muslims

Over 50 million Soviet citizens were Muslims, making up nearly one-sixth of the total population and two-fifths of the non-Russian population. The Muslims, mostly concentrated in the south of the country in republics like Azerbaijan, Uzbekistan, and Kazakhstan, felt that they had more in common with their Muslim neighbors in Iran or Turkey than with the Russians who dominated the Soviet government.

This view was no surprise, as successive Soviet governments had repressed the Muslim faith. The Soviet Union was an atheist state and regarded Islam as a particularly "backward" religion that prevented the assimilation of Muslims into Soviet life and socialist ideology. Many hundreds of thousands of Muslims had been wiped out during

the collectivization of Soviet agriculture under Stalin; one estimate reckoned that up to a third of the population of Kazakhstan was killed during the 1930s. Even in the 1980s, Muslims were still looked upon by some Russians as being backward and inferior.

Independence for the republics

Resistance to Soviet rule swept all parts of the Soviet Union in the 1980s. The Baltic states of Lithuania, Latvia, and Estonia demanded a return to their pre-1940 status as independent states. In the late 1980s it was in the Baltics that anti-Soviet feeling was perhaps the strongest. In August 1989 almost half of the adult population of the Baltics formed a human chain of protest, to back their demand for independence.

Muslim traders in Samarkand, Uzbekistan. Muslims often suffered hardships under Communist rule. One of the questions that arises in the aftermath of the breakup of the Soviet Union is whether the Muslim population may wish to be more closely aligned with neighboring Islamic countries, like Iran.

By 1990, demonstrations in Vilnius, the capital of Lithuania, were drawing crowds numbering a quarter of a million, carrying flags in the Lithuanian colors of yellow, green, and red. Lithuania declared its independence from the Soviet Union and two months later Russian troops were ordered into the country to restore Soviet rule and to seize Communist Party buildings that had been taken over by protesters. While the Russian president, Yeltsin, supported the Lithuanians and held talks with them, the Soviet government imposed harsh economic sanctions, including cutting off 80 percent of its gas supplies. Far from being intimidated by the Soviet response, the other Baltic states began to follow Lithuania's lead. Estonia declared that it was no longer constitutionally part of the Soviet Union.

For a short time, Gorbachev was able to defuse the crisis by using a mixture of economic sanctions and persuasion. He argued that the threat of independence was making it impossible for him to force through economic and political reforms that would benefit the peoples of all the republics.

But although the Lithuanian demands for independence receded in the middle of 1990, they could not be extinguished. By January 1991, there were bloody scenes again in the Lithuanian capital. Soviet troops killed 13 people while attacking demonstrators at the Television Center in Vilnius.

On this occasion, Yeltsin called for Russian troops in the Baltics to refuse to follow orders from the central government. This demonstrated that there was growing discontent in all the republics about the Soviet response to demands for independence. But it also showed that different republics were prepared to help each other on the question of opposing Soviet rule.

Eventually the calls for independence from central Soviet rule were to come from the heart of the Union—from Russia itself. Although the vast Russian republic was the richest in terms of natural resources and industrial development, the average income of Russian workers was low compared to workers in some other republics. In the growing belief that Russians were unfairly subsidizing other republics, calls for independence focused on a growing range of issues—but especially on economic issues. Soon Yeltsin was calling for Russian sovereignty, lending his weight to demands that Russian law should have priority over Soviet law.

Gorbachev had presided over demonstrations, riots, and deaths in Azerbaijan, Armenia, the Baltic states, Georgia, Uzbekistan, the Ukraine, Siberia, and even Russia itself. In August 1991, Gorbachev was planning to sign a New Union Treaty giving much more power to the individual republics. The New Union Treaty would allow the republics to organize their own relations with other states and to set their own taxes. But the treaty was never signed. The August coup attempted to prevent it, but as we see in the final chapter, the events that followed the coup made the treaty look like a minor reform.

On August 24,1989, the fiftieth anniversary of Soviet rule being established in the Baltic states, a human chain of protest was formed across Latvia, Estonia, and Lithuania.

THE SOVIET UNION AND THE WORLD

We have seen in the previous chapters that the Soviet Union had always been a target of hostility from other, non-communist, world powers. Although other countries had criticized the Soviet Union's record on democracy and human rights, they were also concerned that the existence of a successful Communist state might encourage their own populations to reject the capitalist system.

The Cold War

During World War II the Soviet Union had fought on the same side as the Allied armies (of the United States, France, Britain, Canada, Australia, and others) against the German Nazis. The first task was to defeat Germany. But as the war drew to a close, the two superpowers, the United States and the Soviet Union, jockeyed for position in the postwar world order.

In negotiations at the end of the war, the United States and Soviet Union organized the division of Europe. The countries that came to be known as Eastern Europe were placed under Soviet influence while the western European countries continued to develop capitalist economies with the protection and help of the United States. Communist governments took power in the Eastern European countries— Bulgaria, Czechoslovakia, East Germany, Hungary, Poland, Romania, and Yugoslavia. With the exception of Yugoslavia, these countries joined the Warsaw Pact, placing their military affairs under Soviet dominance.

In economic affairs, the Soviet Union set up its own international organization, Comecon, which included all the East European states except Yugoslavia. The Soviet Union supplied these countries with raw materials at prices well below normal world prices. In exchange, they sold

The Soviet Union's last shorter-range missiles were destroyed in October 1989, to comply with the Intermediate Nuclear Forces (INF) Treaty (see page 41).
The pace of nuclear disarmament quickened following the signing of the treaty.

DAILY SKETCH

TUESDAY, OCTOBER 23, 1962 ... 3d.
© 1962, by the Daily Sketch

CUBA

SENSATIONAL MOVE BY KENNEDY

BLOCKADE!

Ultimatum to Kruschev
'Move those missiles'

Pictured in Washington— Kennedy as he said last night: We will not prematurely or unnecessarily risk the costs of world-wide nuclear war in which even the fruits of victory would be ashes in our mouth—but neither will we shrink from that risk at any time it must be faced.

PRESIDENT KENNEDY last nig[ht]
scale blockade of Cuba to stop
missiles there.

He said that Cuba had been turned int[o]
rocket destruction into the heart of Ameri[ca]

Early this morning a defence spokesman said [...]
to sink Soviet ships if necessary to prevent offensive [...]

The President's ultimatum to Cuba and Russia was given in a radio and TV broadcast to the American people. He said:

Within the past week, unmistakable evidence has established the fact that a series of offensive missile sites is now in preparation on the imprisoned island of Cuba.

Two types

The purpose of these bases can be none other than to provide a nuclear strike capability against the Western hemisphere.

The characteristics of these new missile sites indicate two distinct types of installations.

Several of them include **medium range ballistic missiles, capable of carrying a nuclear warhead more than 1,000 nautical miles.**

Each of these missiles is capable of striking Washington, D.C. the Panama Canal. Cape Canaveral. Mexico City, or any other city in the South-Eastern part of the United States, in Central America, or in the Caribbean area.

Additional sites not yet completed appear to be designed for intermediate

range ballistic missiles— capable of travelling more than twice as far—and thus capable of striking most of the major cities in the Western hemisphere — as far North as Hudson's Bay, Canada, and as far south as Lima, Peru.

In addition, jet bombers, capable of carrying nuclear weapons, are now being uncrated and assembled in Cuba, while the necessary air bases are being prepared.

This urgent transformation of Cuba into an important strategic base—by the presence of these large,

long rang[e]
offensive [...]
den ma[...]
constitutes [...]
threat to [...]
security of [...]

This act[ion...]
dicts the [...]
ances of S[...]
both public[...]
delivered. [...]
build-up i[n...]
tain its o[...]
character [...]
Soviet Un[ion...]
or desire t[o...]
missiles on [...]
any other [...]

The size [...]
taking ma[...]

The Cuban missile crisis

In July 1962, American intelligence agencies learned that the Soviet Union was installing nuclear missile bases in Cuba, within 300 miles of the United States.

In October President John Kennedy ordered a naval blockade of Cuba to prevent further missiles and supplies from getting through on Soviet ships, and demanded that weapons already installed be removed. He warned that the United States was prepared to take the risk of all-out war. For a few days in October 1962, the world faced the immediate threat of a nuclear exchange between the superpowers.

Fortunately, once it reached flash point, the crisis was rapidly resolved. Soviet President Khrushchev agreed to dismantle the missile sites and remove the weapons if the United States agreed not to invade Cuba. The Cuban crisis was the most frightening confrontation of the Cold War, but a tense, aggressive relationship persisted between the superpowers until the 1980s.

Gorbachev with Fidel Castro, Cuban Communist leader, in 1989. Under perestroika, *Soviet economic aid to Cuba was rapidly reduced.*

manufactured goods to the Soviet Union. But, more important, their political loyalty was secured.

Soon after the war ended, the relationship between the Soviet Union and the United States worsened. The competing ideologies of communism in the East and capitalism in the West soon brought about a Cold War. In other words, relations were as bad as they could be without war actually breaking out. Each side built more and more weapons, including massive nuclear arsenals. The policy of nuclear deterrence developed, in which both superpowers threatened to use nuclear weapons if the other attacked (so both sides were "deterred" from attacking). Mutual suspicion and fear of losing ground in the arms race led each side to produce increasingly devastating and accurate nuclear and conventional weapons, at great cost to the economies of countries in East and West alike.

Despite lengthy negotiations, the two camps were unable to come to any agreements to reduce their nuclear arsenals. The balance of terror resulting from nuclear deterrence was one of the main factors that kept them from attacking each other directly.

Superpower influence in the developing world
In the developing world, both superpowers used all their available resources to extend their influence. Every region in the world was seen by both sides as a battlefield between capitalism and communism—between American and Soviet influence. Any conflict in the Middle East, Africa or Asia was exploited by both sides to further their own causes.

Whenever a socialist state was established in another part of the world, the Soviet Union provided aid in the form of food, raw materials, manufactured goods, or weapons. When Fidel Castro established a Communist state in Cuba, its economy quickly became dependent on Soviet aid. States like Ethiopia in the Horn of Africa, Vietnam in Southeast Asia, and Angola in southern Africa received Soviet military aid to fight civil wars against anti-Communist forces or to fight other states in the region. Often, this meant giving or selling weapons to countries engaged in bloody wars. For most of the Cold War period the Soviet Union sold more weapons to developing countries than any other nation.

This foreign policy was an additional drain on the Soviet economy. The Soviet Union was selling goods for less than they cost to produce, or even giving them away. Furthermore, while the policy was being followed, it was impossible to improve relations with the United States and other capitalist powers and thus reduce the cost of the arms race.

The end of the Cold War
When Gorbachev came to power in 1985, nearly 1.6 billion people in the world were ruled by Communist governments. That was nearly a quarter of the world's population. But in order to reform the Soviet economy, Gorbachev wanted to cut military spending, improve relationships with the West, and reduce Soviet aid to other countries.

Gorbachev eagerly pursued negotiations to

The Soviet Union sent no troops to the Gulf War of 1990-1991, but gave political support, which was essential to the success of the international alliance against Saddam Hussein of Iraq. Seen here are American troops marching into position in Saudi Arabia in November 1990.

cut nuclear weapons. In December 1989 he signed the Intermediate Nuclear Forces (INF) Treaty banning certain nuclear weapons from Europe. Later he and President George Bush were to sign the Strategic Arms Reduction Treaty (START) cutting the numbers of certain weapons by half. In 1989 he declared that the Soviet Union would reduce its conventional army in Europe by 500,000 troops and 5,000 tanks, paving the way for a treaty on conventional forces in Europe.

Gorbachev also moved to improve relations with other states. He sent his foreign minister to China, in an attempt to mend relations with the next most important Communist state in the world. Relations between the two countries had previously been very bad. He recognized Finland's neutral status in 1989 and visited the Pope in the same year to restore Soviet relations with the Vatican. At the same time he began to reduce Soviet military influence around the world. First, in 1989, the Soviet army in Afghanistan was called home. He also put pressure on the Cubans to withdraw their troops from Angola in southern Africa.

Eastern Europe

The changes that occurred in the Soviet Union also encouraged the anti-Communist revolutions in other East European countries. Throughout the Cold War, whenever dissent had surfaced in these countries, the Soviets had acted to restore or strengthen Communist rule. On two occasions, in Hungary in 1956 and Czechoslovakia in 1968, Soviet troops had been sent to reimpose Communist rule by force. But within a very brief period, between 1989 and 1990, Communist regimes in Poland, East Germany, Czechoslovakia, Hungary, and Romania were swept away in popular protests, and this time the Soviets did not intervene to save them.

Gorbachev's actions signaled a new approach to Soviet foreign policy. He talked of a common European home and sought to play down the ideological differences between the capitalist and Communist worlds. Partly as a result, communists throughout the world were swept from power and, even in Western countries, Communist parties were forced to reconsider some of their most deeply held beliefs.

THE END OF THE UNION

On August 19 , 1991, all of the tensions that had led to Gorbachev's reforms, and that had been exposed and sharpened by *perestroika* and *glasnost*, came to a head as the conservative forces in the government attempted to overthrow Gorbachev in a military coup.

During the night of August 18 the leaders of the army, the KGB, and the Interior Ministry announced that Gorbachev had been taken ill at his home in the Crimea. In reality, they had placed him under house arrest and taken over the government of the country. Tanks drove into the main streets in Moscow to keep order.

But the coup collapsed within days. Gorbachev refused to give in to the demands of the coup leaders. In Moscow, Yeltsin called on the people to act against the coup. Thousands of Muscovites took to the streets to defend the Russian Parliament against the troops. Demonstrations and strikes broke out around the Soviet Union. Many troops refused to obey the orders of their military leaders, and some joined with the protesters in defending the Russian Parliament. In the face of opposition the coup leaders were paralyzed. Amazingly they had not expected any opposition and did not know how to react.

A barricade put up by demonstrators supporting Yeltsin and Gorbachev blocks a Moscow bridge during the coup.

Standing on a tank in front of the "White House," the Russian Parliament building, Yeltsin (third from right) urges Soviets to resist the coup.

Coup countdown: August 22 , 1991

Two days after the beginning of the coup, the crisis came to a head with the confrontation between the army and pro-Yeltsin loyalists outside the Russian Parliament building (the White House) in Moscow:

12:30 A.M. Columns of tanks converge on central Moscow. First barricade broken.

12:45 A.M. Three deaths are reported from Kalinin Avenue, Moscow, but White House resistance continues. Tanks are attacked by the crowds.

5:00 A.M. Demonstrators capture nine armored personnel carriers in Moscow. KGB troops reported on alert.

9:00 A.M. Reports of Soviet officers abandoning the coup. Prime Minister Pavlov, a coup leader, reported ill.

2:15 P.M. Yeltsin tells the Russian Parliament that the coup leaders are trying to leave Moscow by air.

5:00 P.M. Tass news agency says "emergency restrictions" on media have been lifted.

5:10 P.M. The entire coup leadership is reported to have flown out of Moscow.

5:25 P.M. The emergency committee "no longer exists," says Colonel Valeri Ochirov, chairman of Soviet parliamentary defense committee.

6:00 P.M. Yeltsin reported to be on his way to the Crimea to meet Gorbachev.

7:14 P.M. Soviet Parliament formally reinstates Gorbachev as president. He tells Soviet television he is in control again and orders army chiefs to obey only his commands.

Within days the coup crumbled, its leaders were arrested and Gorbachev was back in Moscow.

After the coup, political life in the Soviet Union did not go back to normal. The coup leaders had attempted to stop political and economic reform once and for all. Not only did they fail to do this, but their actions led to a rapid acceleration of the very changes to which they were opposed. Boris Yeltsin and other supporters of immediate reform came out of the situation much stronger than Gorbachev. The coup had failed because—thanks to six years of *glasnost*—people were no longer frightened of the Communist Party. But even though Gorbachev was to be thanked for the

People celebrating the failure of the coup give victory signs beside a huge Soviet flag. New problems and challenges lie ahead.

political reforms, people now wanted reform at a much faster pace. They no longer had patience for Gorbachev's gradual changes.

In the immediate aftermath of the coup, its leaders were arrested and they, and the ministers who had failed to oppose the coup, were replaced by reformers. Provincial leaders who opposed reform were also replaced. The army, the KGB, and the Communist Party itself were regarded by many people as traitors: they were guilty of opposing reform to protect their own interests. They had even proved incapable of forcing their will on an unarmed public.

The Communist Party was suspended in many republics, including the Russian Federation. A few days after the coup, Gorbachev resigned from the Party leadership before leaving the Party and calling on it to disband. Party activities in the armed forces and the security forces were quickly banned and Party property was handed over to local councils. The Party was no longer an important force in Soviet political life. Across the country, statues of Lenin, Stalin, and Marx were pulled down by triumphant demonstrators. The coup had ensured that communism in the Soviet Union was finally and thoroughly discredited.

Republic after republic declared independence from the Soviet Union, setting their own terms for cooperation with each other. In the weeks after the coup, for example, the Baltic republics, Georgia, the Ukraine, and Moldova all declared their independence from the Union. The Ukraine, the second richest republic after Russia, announced that it was to have its own currency and banking system, and even its own army. Moldova, where most of the people are ethnic Romanians and speak Romanian, announced its intention to unite with Romania as one country. On December 22, 1991, a revolutionary agreement was signed by ten of the fifteen Soviet republics creating the Commonwealth of Independent States (CIS). The form and extent of cooperation was essentially left up to individual republics. The Soviet Union had disintegrated.

Danger ahead

By the end of 1991 the economies of the former Soviet republics were in a terrible state. Inequalities of wealth had increased enormously under Gorbachev and looked set to grow as the free market was introduced into the economy. Even the strongest supporters of the market economy knew that their reforms would mean much more economic hardship and inequality for the near future—and much more conflict.

Massive and growing debt would have to be dealt with if the republics were to keep the confidence of Western investors. Inflation was already at 100 to 200 percent and growing, and there were shortages of grain, medical equipment, and power supplies. After the jubilation of defeating the coup, the people throughout the republics again turned their attention to economics rather than politics. A councilor in the Russian city of Ryazan, 140 miles south of Moscow, put it this way: "People are tired of Gorbachev and Yeltsin. What they want is food."

With republics gaining autonomy there was a risk that disagreements over borders and territory might emerge between them. Similarly, there was the danger that people disagreeing with the reforms might become the victims of the same political intolerance that had been the hallmark of the old Communist Party.

In political life, the former Soviet states had no democratic tradition to fall back on. When the Soviet Union was created most people had gone from autocratic rule under the czars to autocratic rule under the Communist Party. Sergei Kolesnik, a Ukrainian politician, put it like this: "There are very few democrats among the top Russians. There are only anti-communists." This was a problem shared by all the republics.

The celebrations that followed the defeat of the coup demonstrated the joy of people liberated from a rigid and totalitarian political system that had brought economic ruin and conflicts of all kinds. But the Soviet peoples were left to face the massive task of building a new political and economic order, a process certain to bring new conflicts to be endured and, overcome.

The end of an era. Lenin led the Bolshevik revolution and shaped the Soviet Union. But here in Vilnius, the capital of Lithuania, Lenin's statue was removed on the day after the failed coup—August 23 , 1991.

GLOSSARY

Arms race   Military competition between countries, in which each tries to match the military strength of the other, resulting in a constant increase in numbers and power of weapons.

Autocratic   The description of a ruler who has total power over a country.

Autonomy   Self rule.

Black market   Illegal trading in goods. The black market operates outside the normal systems and controls of a country's economy.

Bolshevik revolution   The second revolution in Russia, which took place in October 1917, when the Bolsheviks seized power.

Bolsheviks   The revolutionaries who seized power from the interim government in 1917. The Bolsheviks created the Soviet Communist party.

Budget deficit   The financial imbalance that occurs when a government spends more than it receives in income. Total deficit is measured by subtracting income from expenditure.

Capitalism   Political and economic system based on private ownership of the means of production and distribution and a free, competitive market in goods and services.

Cold War   Tension that existed between the United States and the Soviet Union from 1945 until the 1980s, when relations between the two were as bad as they could be without war actually breaking out.

Collectivization   The organization of the Soviet economy in which industry and agriculture were brought under state control. In theory, all means of production were owned by the state on behalf of the people.

Comecon   Abbreviation for the Council for Mutual Economic Assistance, an association for economic cooperation among Communist states under Soviet domination, founded in 1949.

Communism   The political and economic system in which all the people own the means of production and distribution, which are controlled through state planning.

Conscripts   People forced to do military service for a certain period of time, unlike volunteers.

Coup   A sudden seizure of power forcing a change of government in a country, often achieved by illegal or violent means.

Dissident   A person who disagrees with, or is thought to be in conflict with the aims and principles of a government.

Distribution   The movement of goods from where they are produced to where they will be used.

Economic growth   Expansion in a country's economy, usually measured by the rate at which the standard of living rises.

Economic sanctions   Stopping or restricting trade with or aid given to a country.

Elite   A particularly powerful or influential group of people, holding a privileged position because of wealth, education or political power.

Glasnost   Policy of openness in political debate and decision-making in the Soviet Union.

Intermediate Nuclear Forces (INF) Treaty   Signed in 1989, this treaty outlawed a class of land-based short-range and medium-range missiles in Europe.

KGB   The Soviet secret service.

New Union Treaty   Treaty between the Soviet Union and its republics that would have given more power to the republics. It was due to be signed in August 1991 but was interrupted by the attempted coup.

Nonaggression pact   An agreement between countries not to attack each other.

Perestroika   Policy of fundamentally restructuring the economy of the Soviet Union.

Politburo   The main decision-making body of the Soviet Communist Party, formerly the most important committee in Soviet politics.

Pravda   The main newspaper in the Soviet Union. The word *"pravda"* means truth.

Show trial   A trial organized not only with the purpose of bringing evidence against an accused person, but also to demonstrate the power of the state and make an impression on the public.

Socialism in one country   Strategy in which

the Soviet Union decided to follow socialist policies in its own land rather than encouraging or waiting for socialist revolutions to occur in other countries.

Soviet   Russian word for council.

Strategic Arms Reduction Treaty (START) A treaty between the Soviet Union and the United States restricting the numbers of long-range land-based nuclear weapons.

Supreme Soviet   Overall council governing the entire Soviet Union—similar in status to a Western parliament.

White Guards   The military forces that opposed the Bolsheviks from the October revolution in 1917 until their defeat in 1920.

FURTHER READING

For a more detailed look at the last months of the Soviet Union read copies of newspapers between June and December 1991. The best way to do this is to go to your local library where newspapers are held on microfilm. You do not have to read every paper. Instead you can look at the headlines and then you can spot the key reports that are worth reading all the way through. You might want to produce your own timeline of key events in the breakup of the Soviet Union.

There are huge numbers of books on the Soviet Union. Some of the best ones are:

General/history

Anderson, Madelyn K. *Soviet Life: A View of the Peoples of the U.S.S.R.* New York: Franklin Watts, 1989.

Andrews, William G. *The Land & People of the Soviet Union.* New York: HarperCollins, 1991.

Ayer, Eleanor H. *Boris Yeltsin: Man of the People.* New York: Dillon Press, 1992.

Finney, Susan. *The Soviet Union.* Carthage, Il. Good Apple, 1991.

Gillies, John. *The Soviet Union: The World's Largest Country.* New York: Dillon Press, 1985.

Jacobsen, Karen. *The Soviet Union.* Chicago, Il: Childrens Press, 1990.

Keeler, Stephen. *Passport to the Soviet Union.* New York: Franklin Watts, 1988.

Kort, Michael. *Mikhail Gorbachev.* New York: Franklin Watts, 1990.

Stewart, Gail B. *The Soviet Union.* New York: Crestwood House, 1990.

Whitelaw, Nancy. *Joseph Stalin: From Peasant to Premier.* New York: Dillon Press, 1992.

Novels

The works of Alexander Solzhenitsyn paint a picture of life in the Soviet Union, particularly under Stalin. Two of the best are *One Day in the Life of Ivan Denisovich* and *Cancer Ward,* both available in several paperback editions.

For a look into the personal and political lives of women in Russia in the years immediately after the revolution, try the works of Alexandra Kollonati, particularly *Love of worker bees,* also available in paperback.

Films

A number of widely available films also give insights into Soviet history and life. For the 1917 revolutions, see *Doctor Zhivago, Reds,* or *October.* For a more recent look at Soviet life, see *Little Vera.*

INDEX